Daddy's Wisdom:
A Message For My Children

Author Basheer S Jones

This book is dedicated to all children who desperately desire to be loved by their father.

Introduction

As I sit here taking in the mountainous, desert view of Al Ain, (The Spring, a city in the United Arab Emirates) on my 31st birthday I marvel at the journey it took to arrive here. I can't help but to thank God for everything, (Alhamdulillah). I sit here and reflect on His blessings and mercy and cannot control the spasms in my chest; the tears stream down my cheeks. I breathe deeply and nod my head slowly at the majesty of the landscape. I emerge slowly from my seat and turn taking in more of the air which seems thinner than at home. I turn and turn until I am feeling a bit dizzy, this feeling brings a smile and I am immersed in a childhood memory of spinning until I can barely maintain my balance. I'm thankful and appreciative of what God has inspired me to do. Throughout my travels I have reconnected with my developmental years. I pair memories with music, food, and my feelings. They all still exist inside my being even on the top of a mountain, in a foreign country, separated from my family. Where I come from and where I am today are worlds apart. I have just paid from my earned money for this experience. I juxtapose this precipitous view with the concrete jungle streets of Brooklyn. It amazes me as I reminisce about the clawing out of the impoverished struggles of hood life in various locales; Brooklyn, NY, Fayetteville, NC and Cleveland, OH. That epic climb facilitated the travels of today across the globe spreading a message of hope and love. I've lived through so much in these 31 years and it has allowed me to be grateful. I compare the hikes through life and realize the difference in preparation for this expedition and my upbringing. We lived in a community unprepared for the struggles and yet daily we set out with nothing more than sheer grit to get us through. Amazing realizations, and if today was my last day I ponder, what would I want my children to know? I try to bring my children back more than just post cards, trinkets, and gifts. I bring them back colorful stories, tastes, sounds, and smells. I want them to have a proficiency in the cultures that I travel through. I am hopeful that these understandings of human resiliency, battles and effort could help shape their outlook on not only the world, but themselves as well. At this magnanimous moment in my life I have two and a half children. My eldest daughter, Asale is 7, she's sharp, focused and intelligent. My namesake, Basheer Jr. is 5 and has an adventurous spirit, exploring and questioning his surroundings. My strong, dedicated wife is 4 months pregnant with our third child. I have surveyed her caramel dipped silhouette three times impregnated with my children. I envision warriors, poets, activists, generals, encased in her womb. Yet she walks statuesque amongst us mortals. I also have nieces and nephews who I love dearly Nazaha, Khalil, Muhammad, Imani, and Hamzah. I love them all dearly! But at this moment they're still too young to fully comprehend what they need to know about how to be obedient to God, while exploring their dreams and ultimately being successful in this life. The stories will make an impression, but I figured I would create a message that would transcend time and chronicle rites of passage. A missive that could be their guide when they're ready. A piece that would stay with them long after I'm gone. I write this book with joyfulness and melancholy in my heart. I almost feel like it's a going away letter and that makes me despondent. But I'm also full of elation because these words will be read by future generations and be a guiding light for those to come through challenges. This book is written from a father to his innocent children, a husband to his dedicated wife, an uncle to his nieces and nephews. For those children who have lost their father, or never had a relationship with their father, or had a surrogate father; allow my words to comfort you and give you the fatherly advice that you have craved. This message isn't just for my children but all children, those who are young and young at heart. These next seven chapters will highlight what I have come to learn as the most important things you need to know to be positive, fruitful and dignified on every level. In no way am I saying that I've achieved these accomplishments as I went through my tests. Surely, life is a long series of battles of stumbling, learning from mistakes and trials. Life is about moving forward, getting up and making it through. These seven chapters are an attempt to examine my journey thus far and allow the reader to use it as a standard to remind when it's time to measure, evaluate, and learn. If we follow and work towards lofty goals, we will witness amazing things in our lives. Once the student is ready the teacher will appear. Are you ready?

Chapter 1

GOD

God, Can I have a conversation? With the Creator of the Creation. The one who is most loving and most patient. The one who knows everything I'm facing. You know where I'm going, you know where I went. I pray you forgive me when I repent, I pray you forgive me when I do it again. I made a prayer, I know you heard it. I was crying I felt I was worthless, O God I'm just so far from perfect, but You woke me, so I still have purpose

~Basheer Jones

God

Daddy wants you to know that I love you unconditionally, but I will hold you accountable for misbehavior, as God will when you become of age. My soul has been connected to you since before memory was a part of your creation and you grew squiggling inside of your mother. I saw pictures of you in grey, blurry swirls that eventually emerged in hues of tawny caramel. The responsibility that you innocently brought has always been a great inspiration for me. I prayed and loved you every step of the way since knowledge of your presence was made known. You were not an accident but a calculated event pre-ordained by God's decree. Your mother and I married and planned to bring forth babies into this world to guide and nourish through whatever struggles came our way.

I have decided to take a certain path in his life that doesn't include a regulated job where I'm always available at 5:00 like a TV program. A path that has left me alone so often that I crave the solitude that the emptiness provides. I use this time of quietness and serenity to hear my own thoughts and put them in perspective. I realize that It's not easy to be the children of an activist, leader, maverick and passionate visionary. I'm sure while you're growing up you will wish you could've have spent more time with me and I will also mourn the hours we weren't together. I want you to know that daddy had a mission that was bigger than himself. A mission that I had to grow into like a shoe brought too large to accommodate a growth spurt. The sound of the mission in and of itself sounds crazy, "make the world a better place". The plan is to take one thugged out ghetto at a time, and engage its' inhabitants to love God, their children, themselves and their neighborhood. I want you to know that daddy struggled with being balanced in this statement, because I went vacillated trying to make the world a better place while making sure that your world didn't crumble or implode because of that mission. So, I always tried to make sure that our moments were amazing. I pray that I was successful. and even if it wasn't known with a surety that it was my ardent desire.

The first thing that I need you to know is that you must have a relationship with God. This is my number one; most important lesson. A relationship with your Creator, with your Source is of the utmost of importance. I'd like you to compare this relationship to a cellphone, (or whatever gadget is paramount in your life when you read this). Why do we walk around with charger wires or battery bricks in our bags? Because we understand that our phones must be charged to receive the messages that our friends, family, or the universe are trying to send us. When we don't have our chargers and our phone "dies" that becomes a very bad day for us. We become upset and very agitated at the fact that we are no longer connected to the world. As a result of this obsession with what's going on of importance, we keep our chargers in our pockets just to be sure that we don't run into this issue. So, if our phone needs an energy source to remain charged and receive the messages that people are sending then how are we remaining spiritually charged so we are sure that we are receiving clear messages and guidance from our source of energy? You must stay connected with your source so that you may receive the messages that He has for you. If you don't then just like your phone you will be no good for anyone.

I'm not perfect babies. Daddy has made plenty of mistakes and some of them you will read about here. I want you to understand that those mistakes were necessary for growth. While still being a sinner I also learned how to repent, (make Tawba) to God and I ask that you try not to judge my actions and mistakes but the outcomes that I pray you will see. You and I were created for a specific reason and it's up to you to find out your mission and make yourself come true. Mark Twain, an American author said, "The two most important days of your life is when you were born and when you realize why you were born." Throughout life you will constantly be reborn into higher thinking. You'll hear a statement, you'll see something, you'll meet a person, God will speak to you through these natural events or nature and your life will never be the same. If you are growing you will constantly go through births, leaving behind the world (place, thoughts, people) that you once knew. Stay connected to your source! How? Be consistent in your prayers. When people think about prayer, they just think about the physical act of bowing down. By the way, the physical act of bowing down is absolutely necessary. It says that you are closest to God when you are prostrating. Keep your head on the ground in submission. It keeps you aware of where you are in relation to God. You must do that and try your best to never fall short because it is necessary. But prayer or worship is done in many ways. How you treat someone is a form of worship. We say we love God but, yet we treat God's creation like trash. We have no regard for life. Whether it's the life of ants, trees, animals or our fellow human beings. The way we treat God's creation shows what regard we have for the one who created it all and ourselves in relationship to our place on the earth. When we are serving, forgiving or helping people; be aware that pleases God. This way of thinking, behaving, and living helps you to stay connected to your source my loves. Constantly remember that everything around you and in you is all connected to God. Keep as a treasure in your heart and soul that God is the one you must return to. When your mother sends you to the store… doesn't she send you with a specific purpose? Maybe she will have a grocery list for you or she'll tell you what is needed, and you better not forget. So, if your mother has the wisdom to send you to the store for a purpose then without a doubt God has sent us to this earth for a purpose. That purpose is to worship him in everything we do. Remember my children that God is your source of energy and without that guiding light you are already astray, dying or dead.

Chapter 2

Love

"I love you without knowing how, or when, or from where. I love you simply, without problems or pride: I love you in this way because I do not know any other way of loving but this, in which there is no I or you, so intimate that your hand upon my chest is my hand, so intimate then when I fall asleep your eyes close."

~Pablo Neruda, 100 Love Sonnets

Love

Love is one of Daddy's favorite words, Love. It's beautiful to say in every language that I've heard it, (Amour, Hubun, Ai, Lief, Ina Sonki) to name a few. Never allow love to leave your hearts. Everything that you see, and feel is a result of God's Love and His love and mercy to His creation. You were created in love! Look at the trees as they bend through dense forests stretching, curving, twisting to reach their beloved sun. Observe vegetation as they turn and contort to touch the source of light knowing that they will never will but trying anyway. I'm sitting here in my hotel in Dubai looking out the window at the foliage and you can tell that they're in love. Have you seen trees who become void of the sun's love? Other trees, rocks, mountains or clouds block them, and they wither away and die. Look at the impact of love! Look at the impact of too much love though. As you travel through the desert and see thorny cactuses who receive overwhelming love from the sun. God teaches us the importance of balance. It's all Love. We live in this Universe which is a sign of God's love for us. One Love Song sung to us if we take the time to reflect on the signs that God sends us in nature and through people. I want you to live with love. A balanced love. Sometimes love can be imbalanced if you're not careful and it can turn to. Prophet Muhammed (SAW) said, "Love your beloved mildly, perhaps he will become hateful to you someday. Hate whom you hate mildly, perhaps he will become your beloved someday." Love and hate for Allah alone. You will learn what these words mean in time. This lesson is extremely important my love because if you don't love the one who Created you and love what he created in you then you can't love anyone else. That's what we're seeing today in the world. The issue is not that we don't love our neighbors like we love ourselves, we do love our neighbors like we love ourselves, but the problem is that we don't love ourselves! How can you be of benefit to anyone in the world if you don't first love the galaxy that God gave you? It's imperative that you practice positive affirmations often. If you're not careful the world will have you hating yourself my loves. Diabolical individuals have constructed plans to bade you to hate the hue of your skin, shape of your body, features on your face, the sound of your voice, the texture of your hair, your family, your community, and then your very existence. This is not because it deserves to be hated but because you have accepted what the world thinks of you rather than how God has created you and what God knows that you will become. Some people have become powerful, rich and famous for tricking humans to hate themselves. They make comparisons like shaitan. "I am made of fire and he is made of clay".

The world would be a different place if we all loved ourselves and didn't fall for stereotypical symbols of what beauty is. There would be no need for skin whitening cream, liposuction, Botox, weave, makeup, implants, plastic surgery, subcutaneous injections to make plumper rear ends, lips and cheeks, all tools for people who don't see the beauty of what God created them to be in the first so they are not content with who they are so they have accepted this lie that becoming someone else is better for them and the world. When in reality… God created you to be an original and not a copy. You are an original baby! You are not a copy. Even twins are not exact copies of one another baby! Look at the magnificence of the one who created us to serve him and created everything else to serve us. Why? Because every day God or Al Wadud (The Most loving) expresses his love to us. How? Put your hand over your chest. You don't feel that love beating inside of you. And once that stops it's His love that brings us back to Him. It's all love, my love. Live in love. Find things that you can be in love with and give your all too. You have not truly lived until you have experienced nourishing loved. Find something to love. Better yet allow that love to find you and once it does breathe it in. Now smile and allow that feeling to take over your body. There you go. Smile. Doesn't love feel good?

Chapter 3

Faith

Faith is taking the first step even when you don't see the whole staircase.

~ Dr. Martin Luther King, Jr

Faith

Faith is the essence of life baby. Without faith there is no hope and with no hope you become the most dangerous person on the planet. Faith is the belief that there is a force out there greater than you. Faith is the belief that tomorrow will be better than today. Faith is the belief in oneself that no matter how many times you stumble you will get up dust of your clothes and keep pressing on. You're going to need this thing called faith as you travel through your life. It's the only thing that will get you through. The Prophet Muhammed (peace and blessings be upon him) stated that God says, I am to my servant what he thinks I am. That's powerful! If you don't have faith that God will get you through any trial and tribulation, then even once he does, you'll believe it was luck. But know for sure that God is the power behind all things. That statement of God is a powerful statement but if that's heavy think about this. You are also exactly what you think you are. Who are you to you? I'm not talking about what the world thinks of you. I'm asking you who do you know yourself to be? As you go through this life you are going to have to be clear about who you are and who you are not. People are going to try to get you to take other routes instead of the right path. But you must have faith in God and yourself and make decisions that sometime may not be popular in the present but in the long run will be life changing. Faith is the key. You may ask, well daddy how do I strengthen my faith? or How did you strengthen your faith? Number one I want you know that your faith is going to go up and down. One day your faith is going to be so strong and then the next you're going to feel like you can't go on. This is a natural part of life don't get discouraged when this happens to you. And it will happen to you. There are a couple of things that I do that strengthen my faith. Number one I love to read and watch things that show the Magnificence of God. Whether that's reading the Quran, taking a walk-through nature, watching a documentary on bees or ants. I love to see the magnificence of God's creation. When my faith is low, I like to increase in doing good deeds. I'll go visit the sick, feed the hungry, give charity, read to children, take my babies out to dinner, or go speak to people and try to give them inspiration. It's a spiritual secret that I have found in giving. When you give of yourself you also give to yourself. You feel better giving than you do receiving. I've found that when my faith is down doing good deeds increases my faith and makes me feel a whole lot better. Faith to your spirit is what the heart is to your body. Without it you are dead.

Chapter 4

Commitment

If I made a commitment, I stood by that commitment - and try to make it real. Because when you become leaders, the most important thing you have is your word, your trust. That's where respect comes from.

~Michelle Obama

Commitment

To be committed is essential on your journey because it's so easy to give up on your goals. As we go through life, you'll run into a wall that doesn't seem like it can be knocked down and the first thing many people think to do is walk away. Whether that's a business idea or a relationship when many of us face challenges we tend to walk away. There is a beautiful poem called "Don't Quit" that I had to learn, and it says in the poem, "You can never tell how close you are, it may be close when it seems so far. So, stick to the fight when your hardest hit its when things seem worst that you must not quit." You must have the "Don't Quit" attitude because you will never be successful if when challenges come you just walk away. You must be committed to your goals that no matter what wall appears you're going to get through it. Whether you must run through, walk around it or climb over it but no matter what that wall will not be the reason why you quit. On the other hand, daddy doesn't want you to be committed to something that is not the best for you. Don't ever believe that you must fight for something, when you should walk away from it. There is a thin line between patience and stupidity. How do you know? Well baby your daddy never said life was going to be easy. You'll have to figure this out on your own. Only you can truly know what's best for you. If what your committing yourself to brings the best out of you then stick with it but if it's bringing the worst of you then abort mission! Become the type of person that sees things through. Don't become the type of person that is known for easily walking away once there is a small earthquake. Quitters make a habit of finding a reason to walk away but those who are committed to winning find reasons to stay. People who are committed are usually the type of people that others can trust and what can be better than that?

If I made a commitment, I stood by that commitment - and try to make it real.

Chapter 5

Persistence

As long as we are persistence in our pursuit of our deepest destiny, we will continue to grow. We cannot choose the day or time when we will fully bloom. It happens in its own time.

~Denis Waitley

Persistence

I have always admired people who are persistent. Their ability to remain determined to achieve something regardless of any setbacks is certainly commendable. And so, I decided to persist, regardless of how many obstacles I face or how many times that I am told no. Perhaps, I was told "No" to see how dedicated I was. Nevertheless, we must be persistent in what we believe in. We must not become discouraged when things don't go our way. Now don't get me wrong, it is frustrating when things do not go the way that I anticipated but I never consider giving up. I go back to the drawing board and ask myself, "what could I have done differently?" You must be persistent if you're going to achieve your goals. Please do not abandon your vision during adversarial moments. God is redirecting you my love. Take a deep breath and trust Him! Tackling your goals can be very lonely. I don't want you to ever think that I chose my goals over you. My ultimate goal is Heaven. How do I obtain Heaven? By going after what God put inside me, by taking care of my family and being the best human being that I can be. My goal was to always take care of you. I never wanted you to experience what I experienced. I think every parent works hard so their child has a better life than them. The reality is that our children will face their own struggles…and they must! Struggle creates character! I want you to know that you were daddy's first love. I grew up and the only thing I ever wanted was to not be like my father. But once I became a man and a father, I realized that every man can only be what they know how to be. I can no longer hate him or focus on not being him. My focus must be on me being the best me. That's my advice to you my love. Don't focus on not being your father or mother. Just focus on you being the best you. When you focus on that you will be successful! Why? Because it's not hard to be you. It's not hard to just be yourself. It's the easiest task that we have! Everybody else is already taken. It took me years to learn that and I hope with this message it takes you less than that. Daddy loves you with all his heart. The reason I'm writing this book as an expression of my love for you and I pray that you will one day understand. Yes, persistence is the key. You may not get it the first or second time or it may take years for you to understand but you must not quit. True success is not a destination, but it is a journey. What you're looking for may not be at a particular location, maybe it's in the journey that it took to get there. Don't Quit.

Chapter 6

Patience

Patience is not simply the ability to wait - it's how we behave while we're waiting.

~Joyce Meyer

Patience

It's hard to teach something that you have not yet learned to master yourself. Patience is my test my love. I can't speak on this topic in depth at this moment because I battle with this everyday but let me tell you what my elders have said about this topic. You will not win without this. Think about when you plant a seed, does it pop right up as soon as you put it into the ground? Of course, not it's a process. Let me give you an even better example. Imagine a woman who is 4 months pregnant and she's struggling at this stage of her pregnancy. It's tough for her and she is ready for this pregnancy to end. Let me ask you a question what if God answers her plea and allows her to push this baby out at 4 months? Exactly! The baby will come out of her mother premature and the vital organs of the baby will be underdeveloped. The baby will face complications and will have to remain in the hospital under nurse's care. You see the result of the lack of patience. Sometimes you are going to want something to happen right now but maybe if it did it wouldn't turn out the way that is best for you. So, you must have patience and trust that God loves you more than you could ever love yourself. I remember my mother would say, "I want you to have a better life than me." I could not understand at the time why someone would want someone else to have a better life than them. But now I understand. That's the power of love. Unconditional love. Now I share my mother's understanding because I want you as my children to have a better life than me. You must trust that God got you. You must submit to this fact. Because without patience you're going to just drive yourself crazy. There will be moments when you will feel like your drowning but when you submit to God and rest assured that he won't let you drown you begin to float in his love and care. Float in his love my children. Let go. Just let go and you will see what I mean. To be honest you really don't have a choice lol. You will either be patient or go crazy.

Chapter 7

Forgiveness

People are illogical, unreasonable, and self-centered. Love them anyway.

If you do good, people will accuse you of selfish ulterior motives. Do good anyway.

If you are successful, you will win false friends and true enemies. Succeed anyway.

The good you do today will be forgotten tomorrow. Do good anyway.

Honesty and frankness make you vulnerable. Be honest and frank anyway.

The biggest men and women with the biggest ideas can be shot down by the smallest men and women with the smallest minds. Think big anyway.

People favor underdogs but follow only top dogs. Fight for a few underdogs anyway.

What you spend years building may be destroyed overnight. Build anyway.

People really need help but may attack you if you do help them. Help people anyway.

Give the world the best you have, and you'll get kicked in the teeth. Give the world the best you have anyway." — Kent M. Keith, The Silent Revolution: Dynamic Leadership in the Student Council

Forgiveness

An elder said to me, "Basheer you must let the prisoner go... in order to be free. You must release the anger that resides in you or you will forever be imprisoned by it." To be honest baby this is something that daddy battles with. Forgiving those who I have felt done me wrong. Daddy holds grudges. If it was a contest baby daddy would definitely win or lose depending on how you look at it. I love very hard. Maybe it's the Scorpio in me lol. I love very hard and when the person I love hurts me it's hard to get over it. The reason why I'm expressing this to you is because I don't want you to lose the time that I have lost being angry with someone else. I was the prisoner of the jail I created. and I remained in this jail even though at any moment I could've walked right out. Babies I beg you to be a person of forgiveness. How could we expect God's forgiveness but were not able to forgive his creation? I'm talking to myself first. I've lost a lot of time being angry with others. Daddy has also lost good friends and good people because of it as well. Growing up, daddy had a lot of anger. I was angry that I didn't have any relationship with my father, we were homeless, no money, bad neighborhoods, no food some nights and I felt hopeless. Why? Because I would watch my mother cry and I couldn't do anything about it. I would try so hard to make my mother happy but there was nothing I could do to change our condition. It wasn't a good feeling. Even to think about it right now makes me sad. So, daddy was angry and always ready to fight. I didn't know any other way to express this feeling of hopelessness. I'm so thankful to God that my anger didn't get me killed. But to be honest my anger was also my inspiration. It inspired me to make sure that you would never experience what daddy went through. I have forgiven my father because he could only love the way he knew how. I pray for him and you every single time that I pray. Babies don't waste time like your father has done being angry for a long time with people. Because guess what? Because the anger that you have only affects you! Going to sleep and waking up with this feeling inside you will not help a bit. Here are a few tips that you can do when you get angry. 1. Sit down! lol! This is important! When your angry don't you feel yourself getting hot? Almost like your blood is boiling? Remember this, Heat rises. In your school you've probably have heard people say when there is a fire "Stop, Drop, and Roll." The lower you get the cooler it is. So, when you get angry if your standing up then sit down. If your sitting down, then lay down. 2. Drink some water or put some water on your face. When firemen come to put out the fire, they don't use fire right? They use water. It will cool you down. 3. Lastly, walk away because nothing will be accomplished when your angry. Once again Daddy is still working on these things but please learn from Daddy's mistakes.

Closing Remarks

Daddy loves you more than words can ever express. You all are the seeds that daddy has left to make this earth a better place. I want you to blossom into amazing trees that benefit the world through your fruit or the comfort of your shade. Don't be the type of tree that benefits no one. Your success is not how much money you make, car you drive or clothes you wear. Your success is measured by how many people you help uplift. Through your words and actions. Through your love. Love Babies. I want you to love even when others don't show it. If you don't see love, then you're not looking in the right direction. Look at how the Sun loves God. The Suns light reflects God's light. The Sun loves God so much that he shines on us even though we can't do anything to repay him. He shines on us because of his love for God. I want you to be like the Sun. Shine on others even if they can't do anything for you. Shine on them to repay the debt to God for shining through you. Shine babies! Be the light in the darkest nights! Love
babies! Do everything in Love. I love you all! Always remember that! When daddy has left this Earth and you miss me just put your hand on your chest. That's me. How? Because it's you! And you and I are one. Love you!

Made in the USA
Middletown, DE
10 March 2022